Cyril the Squirrel

and the Christmas Jumper

Story by Jill Watton

Illustrations by Charlotte Firbank-King

Cyril the Squirrel and the Christmas Jumper

by Jill Watton

All proceeds from the sale of this book will be donated to St John's Hospice, North Lancashire and South Lakes.

Produced in aid of

St John's Hospice

ISBN: 978-1-0369-2523-9

Illustrations by Charlotte Firbank-King

Editing and book design by Lana Hunneyball

Dedication

In honour and remembrance of my wife, Jill Watton.

You gave me what was yours and I will keep this where a second is a thousand years, and every moment shared with you is my forever and always, in which I was blessed beyond measure.

With special love, your husband, Gary.

Isaiah ch 40 v 31 (your favourite scripture):

But those who hope in the Lord will renew their strength, They will soar on wings like eagles, they will run and not be weary, they will walk and not faint.

Romans ch 8 v 28 (prophesied)

And we know that in all things God works for the good of those who love Him, who have been called according to His purpose.

Once, in a cosy hedgerow in a wild, wonderful garden, lived a little squirrel named Cyril with his mum and dad.

Cyril lived a happy life darting up tree trunks and searching for tasty nuts.

On sunny afternoons, he lay on branches and watched the birds swoop and soar.

At the far end of the garden stood an old, ramshackle house. The paint was faded, and rusty drainpipes clung to the crooked walls.

Cyril loved scampering
up the twisty ivy and
leaping across the sagging
porch roof.

But more than anything, he loved peeking through the windows. There was a family inside – a mum, a dad, and a little girl.

"Be careful, Cyril!" his mum would shriek. "It's not safe – come back!"

Cyril always listened, though it made him sad. The family seemed to have so much fun.

Much more fun than scratching for acorns and sniffing for berries.

"Don't dawdle, Cyril," Mum scolded. "We haven't stored enough for winter, and it's going to be a cold one."

But Cyril couldn't help himself. He was a bit of a dreamer and always full of questions.

"Dad, why do we hide our winter stash in so many different places?"

"Because, son, if we don't, it might get raided."

"Raided? But who – ?"

"Other squirrels and chipmunks, robins and mice – they'd snatch it up in a thrice!

Even foxes and shrews! In winter, everyone's looking for food," Dad said.

Cyril pouted. "It's all work and no fun."

Mum shook her head. "One day, Cyril, your adventuring ways will bring us trouble."

Whenever he got tired of foraging, and Mum and Dad weren't looking, Cyril would bound off through the undergrowth, back to the ramshackle house, and scoot up its wonky gutters.

He couldn't help it.
He just loved peeking through those windows.

One day, the little girl saw him on the windowsill. “Look, Mum,” she said. “It’s that squirrel again! I think he likes me.”

She tiptoed a bit closer, expecting Cyril to dart away, but he stayed put.

The next day, he came again. This time, she opened the window a crack. “Hi, I’m Daisy,” she whispered. “I’ll come outside and play with you later.”

She didn’t expect Cyril to understand, but he did.

His heart leaped, and he felt warm and fuzzy inside. He tried to say, “I live in the hedgerow at the end of the garden,” but it came out as a chattery purr.

Daisy kept her promise. She stood by the hedgerow and looked all around. "Squirrel, where are you?"

Mum and Dad were fixing the nest. "I wish we'd found a tree hollow for winter," Mum chattered anxiously. "They're safer and warmer."

"They're all taken. But our hedgerow nest is strong," Dad said, testing the matted wall of woven leaves and twigs. "We'll be fine."

Mum and Dad didn't hear Daisy calling, but Cyril did.

As soon as Mum and Dad weren't looking, he dashed off.

When Daisy saw him, she clapped with delight, and they played the long summer day away.

When Cyril got home, Mum and Dad were cross.
"We were worried," Dad said.

"I was playing. I should have asked, but I thought you'd say no."

Dad nodded. "Playing is important. Next time, tell us where you're going, okay? We could all make more room for fun."

"But we must save our energy for winter," Mum grumbled.

Dad smiled. "Fun can ease our worries."

Summer slipped into autumn. Green leaves turned to fiery orange and rust and began to fall. Flocks of birds gathered on the wires getting ready to fly South for the winter.

The days grew colder, and the sun set earlier. Daisy mostly stayed indoors, reading or knitting with her mum.

Daisy looked happy, but Cyril felt lonely.

Soon it was too cold to visit. Cyril and his family spent a lot of time sleeping in their nest, only venturing out to fetch food from their stashes.

One morning, Cyril woke to find the garden covered in a bright blanket of snow.

He could barely see Daisy's house and worried she had forgotten him.

The days got even colder. Huge white snowflakes tumbled in the icy wind. "Winter will never end. I'm so bored," Cyril whined. Then he felt guilty. Their hedgerow home was safe and warm.

But Cyril's dad frowned. "This winter is getting worse. We need a warmer nest."

"What?" Mum squeaked. "How ridiculous. We can't move away from our food stores. And it's too cold to take chances."

Fear gripped Cyril.
What? Leave Daisy?

He squinted through the snow-tangled sky hoping for a glimpse. The house was shut tight. What if she'd moved away, or fallen in the snow and was freezing to death?

"Cyril, you'll freeze out there," Mum shrieked. "Get back here at once!" But before she could stop him, Cyril bolted outside and raced across the garden. "I must see if Daisy's alright."

Panting, he reached the house. His sharp claws, usually perfect for climbing trees, slipped on the icy drainpipes. The howling wind nearly toppled him from the porch roof, but he finally reached his favourite window.

Balancing on the ledge, Cyril peered through the glass.

Daisy and her family were decorating a tree with shiny baubles. They wore red and green jumpers with snowman and reindeer designs.

How he wished he could be inside, helping.

Oh yes, he thought.
It's Christmas.

Those jumpers must be what Daisy and her mum had been knitting.

"How nice for them. While we freeze under the hedgerows, they're all snug in their fancy human nests," he mumbled grumpily.

Then a terrible thought struck Cyril. What if Daisy wasn't his friend anymore? What if she'd never been his friend? What if it was his dad's fault they didn't have a better home?

“It’s not fair!” He stamped his foot – and slipped. Squealing, he clung desperately to the ledge.

Daisy ran to the window. “It’s that squirrel!”

Cyril got such a fright that he lost his grip. A powerful gust roared through the garden and flung him from the roof.

“Heeelp!” he yelled, his voice swallowed by the howling wind.

Cyril landed with a soft thud in the snow. He shook himself off and ploughed through the blinding whiteness towards home. With each step, the cold burrowed deeper into his bones, and home never seemed to get any closer. *I'm such a fool. I'll never make it in time.*

Bedraggled and frozen through, he stumbled into the nest. Mum pulled him into her arms, trembling. "We were worried sick. What were you thinking?"

"He's home and safe, and that's what matters." Dad said. Cyril snuggled into Mom as tightly as he could, feeling safe and warm.

That night, Cyril dreamed of Christmas jumpers and cosy fires with Daisy. But when he woke, he remembered she was not his friend.

"I'm going to sleep until spring. Wake me when you hear the blackbirds and blue tits sing," he said.

Dad frowned. "But son, we need your help fetching food. What's wrong?"

"Nothing. Just leave me alone." Cyril curled up, pushing away dreams of warmth and friendship.

Next morning, Cyril woke as Daisy's voice drifted into his dreams. *Go away,* he thought, snuggling deeper into his sleep. *I'm not ready to wake up.*

The soft voice called again, and he opened one eye. Something blue and green flashed against the snow.

Startled, Cyril sat up and crept from the leafy gap in their nest.

It was Daisy! She smiled broadly, holding up a tiny red jumper. “I knitted one for each of you. Now you won’t be so cold.”

Cyril could hardly believe his eyes. “Mum, Dad!” he called. “Look what Daisy made for us!”

Cyril felt bad for his unkind thoughts about Daisy. "I hope we can have fun together again when spring comes," he chirruped, and she seemed to understand.

"I'd better get back. See you soon," she said, then turned and headed back through the snow.

Mum stroked Cyril's head. "It seems I was wrong, young man. Your adventuring ways have brought us good fortune after all."

And to this day, if you spot a flash of red among the squirrels in the trees, look a little closer – you might just see one wearing a beautifully knitted Christmas jumper, thanks to a very special friend.

The end

Printed in Dunstable, United Kingdom

67871668R00020